seeing is everything

angie allen

seeing is everything

written and arranged
by angie allen

ISBN: 9781980904922
cover & section art by pride nyasha

instagram @angie.l.allen
instagram @pride_nyasha

dedication

to jude and noah, you will forever be my little
princes. i pray you stay wild and you stay free
for inside of you are pieces of me.

to debbie, thank you for your unfailing support,
your friendship, your ride or die spirit and for
believing in me at a time when no one else did.

to dally, may you always know how three little
words changed the course of my life, how the
smallest of words can leave the largest of
marks. thank you endlessly for your friendship,
your perspectives, and for giving living pieces
of yourself so graciously.

to friends and family - even those no longer a
part of my life - thank you for the privilege of
your company along this journey. you've
unknowingly helped shape the me i was
meant to be.

to my readers, thank you for allowing my
words to have a place to rest, for my heart to
have a home in your hands, and for your
endless support. these words are for you, please
know you are never alone.

- if seeing is anything

know it is *everything.*

contents

seeing is everything

i am not lost i am in between blooms.

winter

angie allen

late bloomer

hearts need space to open
to break into pieces away
from the maddening crowd

a place to lay in the darkness
until the noise settles
a place to grow into ourselves
and out of others

i am not lost i am in
between blooms

i was always going to bloom
again with or without you.

seeing is everything

the becoming

i am pressed
between the
pages of

who i was and
who i am yet
to become.

angie allen

wanted

when i said
i wanted all of
you i meant the
broken pieces too.

seeing is everything

ash & clay

we are everyone
we have ever loved

we are pieces of their pieces
we are ash and we are clay

we are molded by moments
haunted by memories
of those never meant to stay

yet we gave
we lived and
we loved until
our dying day.

angie allen

...i make homes

out of hurricanes
things just passing
through.

seeing is everything

temporary resident

my hands wrapped
around myself never
felt much like home
no matter how hard
i tried

and so like a gypsy i
have traversed this
earth in search of the
familiar
in search of a home
and the problem
is always the same

i make homes out
of hurricanes things
just passing through.

angie allen

masquerade bawl

i never had a chance
to believe in monsters

mine were made of
flesh and bone
things masquerading
around as people.

seeing is everything

bruised, but sweet

perhaps the bruised
fruit is the sweetest
because it had sense
to be still and wait

and so i will make a
church out of this skin
until patience seeps
from my scars like honey.

fine print

please hear me
when i say

if it comes with
conditions walk
the other way.

seeing is everything

holy

i was always in one
piece until i wasn't

you only notice
you're broken
when you are no
longer whole

when the light is
shining through
where w|hole|
once stood.

angie allen

hearts, homes, bones

the broken things
we try to hide yet
carry with us
deep inside.

seeing is everything

perennial

and just like the universe
growth is forever expanding
within us

i find myself growing
in the small seemingly
insignificant moments
i am healing there

if not for the growth
where would we be
if not for the seasons
how would we change?

angie allen

...breaking isn't an option

it drops us to our knees
the choice is what we
do with the dirt.

seeing is everything

build or bury

that's the choice we have
when we are on our knees
clenching dirt between our
white knuckled fists
it doesn't matter what broke us
what matters is what we
do with the pieces

burying them is easy when
you're already on the ground
don't go for easy just because
it's within your grasp - rebuild

when your whole world has
been broken and you're cutting
your tired fingers on the jagged
pieces at your feet keep rebuilding
push through the fatigue

one day you will look back at the
slight scars on your fingers and be thankful
those scars saved you from being buried
those scars let the light back in.

angie allen

veiled

my soul
craves
more than
this lie.

seeing is everything

flow

i cry if nothing
more than to
taste your name
on my tears.

25

angie allen

ode to dad

the st. johns river was silent that day
minus the water lapping against the
shore as other boats passed us by

in order to fish with my dad i had to
be quiet but i can swallow words when
necessary

so it caught me off-guard when he said

"you gotta be careful of that stuff
it'll damn near kill ya."

he was staring off into the distance looking
at his fishing line as i asked what stuff

one word one single word was all he
muttered, "love."

i know now he was in that place in his mind
that place he stored all his thoughts and
feelings the things he only revealed when he
was deep in a bottle of jack or jim or
jameson

seeing is everything

i know this place too now that i'm older
the last time i saw him we visited that place
together - just him and me and a bottle of brown

he only talks about her when he's near gone
and he doesn't say much

"i loved her and," i grabbed his hand as tears
streamed down his face

he didn't say anything else except

"i loved her, and it damn near killed me."

angie allen

floating

my heart longs
to be weightless
in a way that
only water fully
comprehends.

seeing is everything

haunt

i'll never
outrun
my ghosts

not when
my thoughts
haunt me
the most.

angie allen

burn with me

it is heavy
this love i carry
inside my ribs
this fire inside
my bones
wondering if
i'll die with it
all alone.

seeing is everything

howl your truth

in the end the truth
always comes out
it refuses to be hidden
demands to be heard

it's fought for died for
and some of the rare
ones bleed their truth

this five letter word
ignites fires - so do it
set your truth free

after all truth is
something you howl
not hide.

angie allen

abandoned

i need only
look rib deep
to know love
once lived
here and
yet still
there is beauty
in the abandoned.

seeing is everything

spent

i am a giver who continues to give
in a world full of takers who
continue to take

yet still i will continue to
give until i have nothing left
until i am emptier than empty

i would then try to give my
emptiness and the takers
would still take and ask

is that all you have left to give?

angie allen

release

there is
strength
in this
letting go
it's how we heal
it's how we grow.

seeing is everything

welcome

i have fallen a long
way from myself
for once i'd like to
fall into myself and
feel at home

why is it so hard to
make a home out of
this skin these bones?

angie allen

western skies

i feel stuck in between
the holding on and
the letting go

lost or maybe just a
delayed found

like the few weeks
after fall but before
winter sets in and the
leaves are restless

there are no more
seasons for us
you are stuck at
winter and i am
searching for the sun.

seeing is everything

vein love

we carry lifetimes
inside our veins
a mosaic of memories
a collection of moments

you became a part of
what flows within me
a stream of time and
space where it bends
in all directions

i can trace you back
to the start
back to the beats of
my broken heart

one feel of my pulse
and i know you still
remain under the surface
inside my veins.

angie allen

shine on

you wear your heart
on your sleeve like
the sun wears shine

to show the world
you are made of light

keep shining
it's how we find
the good ones.

seeing is everything

misfits

there is beauty in
the broken
the fallen
the forgotten
the abandoned
the misunderstood

they shoulder heavy
hearts that beat with ink
stories pulsing in their veins
tired eyes blinking dreams
brokenness dripping from
their lips and wings

i see you and god
you are nothing short
of beautiful.

angie allen

…don't you see

i say your name in
every word it's just
spelled differently here.

seeing is everything

your name xxxxx

i see your name in everything
is it any wonder when i write
you bleed through the ink

your name is written in the stars
all the ones i've wished upon and
all the ones i have yet to still

i see it on the backs of butterflies
wondering if they once graced
my stomach with your name on
their wings

i feel it in the falling rain and see it
in every shade of green it brings
i cry as i often do and i can taste
it on my tears

don't you see i say your name
in every word it's just spelled
differently here.

angie allen

history of us

i trace the carved
hearts on trees left
behind by lovers

i run my fingertips
over their chiseled
edges and i don't
know why but i cry

perhaps it's the power
of two people that said
we loved and we were here

and i cry because
i want to say

i know and i see you.

seeing is everything

story book eyes

sad eyes tell the
most beautiful
stories and she
had the saddest
eyes of them all.

angie allen

time

allow it for yourself
become seasons
upon seasons
if you must.

seeing is everything

precious medals

i am a soldier of war wearing battles
on my sleeve and rusted medals on my heart
i harbor old wounds and scars that run
as deep as trenches etched inside my soul
the very trenches where you callously cast me aside
a calculated casualty as if i were nothing more
than a pawn in your front line

i can't right the wrongs you committed yet
i can grasp this steely pen with my trigger finger
stare down the barrel of truth

and write, and write, and write

until i have riddled these pages with bullets of ink
until i have bled you out of my narrative

i am better for having loved and lost
stronger for having walked away
and in the end the medal weighing heaviest on
my heart and the one i bare the proudest is

t r i u m p h.

angie allen

palpable

my mind is drowning
in an ocean of your
words and i don't
resurface for air

i'd rather breathe
them in until i can
taste your thoughts
like ink on my tongue.

seeing is everything

myself, growth, unhappiness

things i am
no longer
apologizing for

i told myself
to find happiness
and grow there
so i did.

angie allen

love of my life

there is no
further i could fall
six feet under couldn't
keep you from me
not even a little
not even at all.

seeing is everything

heartfelt

there is a difference
between something
being artfully contrived
and something
contrived artfully
only one of these
stems from the heart.

angie allen

dressing up sadness

smile she said
jesus loves you

in that moment
i realized dress up
and fairytales went
hand-in-hand

i played the part
we southern girls
learn real young

how are you?
fine (smile)

yes what?
ma'am (smile)

seeing is everything

stand up straight
don't slouch
(smile)

turn that frown
upside down
(smile, smile)

southern hospitality
served with a (smile)

i've been smiling
through tears for
more years than i
care to count

all (smiles) aside.

angie allen

two faced

we were
strangers
once

now we are
nothing more
than strangers
with familiar
faces.

seeing is everything

illusive

memories echo their
stories loudly
and chase closure
with bare hands.

…i hate this
about myself

but i can't help falling
for the broken and beautiful
i couldn't help falling for you.

seeing is everything

beautifully broken

i hate this about myself detest it really
this attachment to all things broken
perhaps it's because my heart was broken
long before it knew how to beat whole
or perhaps we have this intrinsic desire
to search for those that are reflections
of who we are inside

whatever the reason i have always
had a heart for all things broken
especially people

there is something you can see
in their eyes something that is missing
it can't be smiled through
the broken understand the pain
the darkness the struggle the everything

of all the broken things i've come across
you are the most beautiful and
i'm attached to your broken.

angie allen

star boy

your sad eyes
carry a universe
of untold stories

and yet you hold
their pain as the
sky holds the stars

beautifully hidden
in plain sight

i don't always see it yet
i know it's always there.

seeing is everything

changing tides

we can unravel
with such speed
when unseen tides
pull us apart

so forgive me if
i hold on just a
little (too) tight.

angie allen

footprints

everywhere we go we are the
footprints of where we've been
we carry our past our history on
the spines of our paper backs
and sometimes it's the things we
don't choose that make up who
we are

like the city we are born in
the family we are born into
the towns that shape and raise us
the things we don't ask for and the
things we never saw coming

it's these seemingly insignificant
things that help mold and shape us
so that literally everywhere we go
we are the footprints of where we
have been and where we still have
yet to go.

seeing is everything

the climb

some days anxiety
builds the tallest of
walls inside of me

the wanting to scale
them is always there

the strength
however is not.

angie allen

....there is no such

thing as a
dead end
when you
have wings.

seeing is everything

broken things still fly

on days like today when i feel
like the word shattered
when i am watching the rain fall
and release itself in only ways
water can seemingly do
to feel everything all at once yet
release it so effortlessly
it's on days like this i have to remind
myself that what appears to be a
dead end isn't really the end after all
that maybe it's more like a u-turn
in the making
then once i round the corner and
head in the other direction i smile
because i realize there is no such thing
as a dead end when you have wings
dead ends may clip a pair of wings
but they grow back all the same
broken things still fly.

angie allen

the sky & you

things i
only dream
of touching.

seeing is everything

mute

it's all the words you
didn't say that i hear
the loudest that hurt
the deepest

all that you never said
is all that i ever hear

unspoken words leave
unspeakable scars.

.

angie allen

...if not for the

sake of clarity
what is the
breaking for?

seeing is everything

50 shades of clarity

it's taken longer than expected yet i've
come to appreciate that things and people
in this life will knock me down
it's a vicious cycle of

break
breaking
broken

yet in each layer of decent i find the
most beautiful shades of clarity
if not for the clarity what is the
breaking for

truth is i like what i've broken into
and i've never been one to withhold
credit where credit is due so i guess
i have two final words to say

thank you.

angie allen

love

it's a four letter word
we both spit and swallow

that crazy beautiful place
where we can be both lost
and found at the same time

perhaps there is no singular
definition for something with
infinite possibilities

maybe that's the point
in the end it's all we've got.

seeing is everything

golden

silence speaks
our language
when the only
thing left to
say is nothing

sometimes
saying nothing
is everything that
needs to be said.

angie allen

flood light

ink is the flashlight
to my darkest parts
to those thoughts lodged
in the deepest corners
of my ribs

although i may not be
able to form the words
past my teeth that doesn't
negate their existence

sometimes the only release
i have is through my pen
i use it to illuminate my heart

ink is the flashlight to
my darkest parts
i yield to it's light if
only to find my
way back home.

seeing is everything

wide open spaces

i love with my
heart wide open

perhaps that's why
it's so easily broken.

angie allen

rooted

to look within
is never to be
without

for inside the
roots of me
i carry all i
am yet to be.

seeing is everything

run

when your monsters
tell you about theirs

it's time to get out
from underneath
the bed.

angie allen

…look at us dead
on and we are

the fallen
the barren
the tree green
with no leaves.

seeing is everything

dead on

it's dying from the inside out
this tree rooted in my front yard
half autumn half winter
half alive but mostly dead

with only the left eye i see her still
green with the rain of summer
with the right she is heavy with
the weight of winter

i look away for she is like me
and maybe like you too
look at us with your left eye and
we are all the shades of green after the rain
look at us with your right and we are
crimson and scarlet the fallen leaves
at your feet

look at us dead on and we are
the fallen
the barren
the tree green
with no leaves.

angie allen

shadows

they are born of light
yet reflect the night
and still only in our
shadow are we ever
truly reflected whole

not all moments are
teaching moments
but i know one thing
for sure

light doesn't lie.

seeing is everything

lines

some guys
cross them
other guys
walk them.

picked

my heart
is an
open
wound
ripe with
healing.

seeing is everything

after life

i want a
love that
transcends
the dashes
between
these dates
and a life
that made
the dashes
count

in life and
in love i'd
be just fine
to know that
i was yours
and you
were mine.

angie allen

bottoms up

you swallowed
autumn and
let me

fall
fall
fall

from your eyes
like leaves.

seeing is everything

taken

i can be anything
and yet there are days
when all i want is to be

someone's someone.

angie allen

paused

they say time will tell
as if it speaks a language
we can understand

if i'm honest time
doesn't speak in
tongues only

in measures
in beats
in moments
of singularity

you either feel them
or you don't
truth is time never
spoke our language
it just didn't beat for us.

seeing is everything

prologue

let my whispers
drown yours
as we make love
to the quiet chaos
of their chords.

angie allen

i am bare yet not without the will to bloom.

seeing is everything

f a l l

angie allen

emerge

and today i wear hope
like a february tree

her naked branches
offering the first signs of
spring as if whispering

i am bare yet not without
the will to bloom.

seeing is everything

unapologetic

i've been told

i am intense
i spill over the edges
i am simply too much

and yet how could i
ever be sorry for

living so incredibly loud
loving so incredibly hard
feeling so incredibly deep?

angie allen

the silver lining

and some days
we hold hurt
like the clouds
hold the rain

until we can't.

seeing is everything

dying to live

no i never did
fear it death i
mean

rather i feared a
life not worth
dying for.

angie allen

the in between

i wanted to find you on
the other side of whole
i wondered what you looked
like wondered if you sounded
the same
would your laugh sound fuller
would your eyes still hold the rain
would your smile still taste the
same despite the pain
and then i realized we are all of
the spaces in between ourselves
we are where we have been and
where we have yet to go
we are who we have met and
who we have yet to know
always half broken never
really whole
broken has a way of shining
on the other side of whole
and i found you in all the
spaces in between.

seeing is everything

logistics

show me your pain
and i will show you
where poetry resides
there are no places

too dark
too deep
too unwanted
that my words
can not reach

for where there is
pain there is poetry.

angie allen

rest in pieces

i fall hard
and all at
once

i simply don't
know how to
fall for you in

p i e c e s.

seeing is everything

new beginnings

all i ever
needed
was another
reason to
begin again.

angie allen

bare - a daisy with no petals

naked - crushed yellow center

truth - the shame was not mine

bare, naked, truth
scattered seeds grow
the strongest roots and
bloom wildly at will.

seeing is everything

monsters

i was never
scared of the
ones under my
bed just the ones
inside my head.

angie allen

a haiku, assumptions

my mistake when i
asked for a heart to heart i
assumed you had one.

seeing is everything

felt

at times to feel
anything

is simply
everything.

angie allen

judgemint

if our words came
in flavors i'd like to
believe we would
think twice about
the bitter taste of
judgement on our
tongues.

seeing is everything

lost and found

oh, the
places
we hide
in order
to find
ourselves.

angie allen

released

there is something to
be said for the fallen
they never doubted
their ability to fly.

seeing is everything

poetic alchemy

there are cavities in
me that ache in ways
hunger could never fill

i am tired in places
sleep could never
dream of waking

yet when i write
when i open up all the
pieces of my heart and
i bleed into those spaces

the release is alchemy
to my bones and poetry
to my soul.

angie allen

raise your voice

i was afraid of who i
was underneath it all
yet i gave way to my
fears to become myself
how can you fear the
very thing you were
destined to become

i learned my mouth was home
to purpose and intent and i was
intent on screaming with every
fiber of my being until i heard my
own voice amongst the choir

i had been taught that by our
voice we would be known by
something higher

then surely by the same token i
would recognize my voice
when i heard it ring true
i would sing until i was hoarse
in doing so i would find my way
back to me the one i was destined to be.

seeing is everything

inside out

i long to wear
my shell the way
it wears my skin
exposed for the
naked eye to see.

angie allen

rhetorical question

between us there exists a canyon
of all the things you will not say
and all the things i can not ask
you're silent i'm stubborn and
untold stories hang in the balance

funny the things you see the things
that are only there because you
want them to be

turns out you're not so good with words
turns out i'm not so good with questions
turns out we're not so good for each other
please, since when did that ever matter
to anyone?

p.s. for the record that's
just a rhetorical question.

seeing is everything

day break

it was in the way
you spoke silence like
a native tongue that
i realized you had
moved on

much like the moon
does at dawn with
little indifference
and without saying
goodbye.

angie allen

heavy petal love

give me a
love soft
enough for
petals yet
strong
enough
for roots.

seeing is everything

glass menagerie

he said he was looking
for a message in a bottle
and i naively assumed he
meant a message scrawled
on weathered paper
the kind that washes up on a
sandy beach with a cork topper

in time he amassed a menagerie
of bottles and it turned out the
message he was looking for wasn't
in that bottle or the next one or the
one after that

one day the message finally
arrived and it simply said

p.s. you'll never find what you are
looking for here the message was
never in the bottle.

angie allen

middle ground

beginnings
and endings
have their place

i just prefer
the spaces
in between.

seeing is everything

made of dirt

we build castles
out of people in
our minds shaping
them larger than life

how utterly disappointing
when they turn out to be
just like everyone else.

angie allen

midnight swim

i can still taste your
soft whiskey stained lips
feel the weight of your
body pressed against mine
hands in my hair
the smell of salt
on your skin

the night spilled shadows
from your eyes and i took
a midnight swim.

seeing is everything

parched

freedom is relative
to where you are and
where you are not
to where you have
been and the miles
yet still to go

it's an elusive curious
mirage i walk towards
wondering if the gap
between the two will
ever be bridged.

angie allen

the sum of things

when doing nothing
is no longer an option
you realize you have
to do something

those somethings might
look like a whole lot of
nothings but keep going

it's the journey you take
to make your somethings
count.

seeing is everything

speak in tongues

and if you would
speak to me in
mosaics

in a language
where broken pieces
are given a chance to
be loved whole

i have a heart
for tongues that
speak in scars.

angie allen

...they say broken

hearts break hearts
but the truth is your
words broke mine.

seeing is everything

broken english

the truth is we see things how
we want to see them at the time
and once we see them for what
they are there is no going back

the only thing we ever exchanged
were words - words separated by
more miles than syllables

they were an easy thing to fall for
and yet now i wonder what i ever
saw in them at all

when the colors fade they drain
to black and white back to
pure sight

they say broken hearts
break hearts but the truth is
your words broke mine.

angie allen

constellation tracer

you come to me clearest
on crisp autumn nights
the bonfire heating my skin
where your fingers once
traced the stars

and i wonder do i come
to you anymore even a
little even at all?

seeing is everything

wanting hands

i wish i could be
so free of you
the way you have
become of me

how do you do that
be so free of someone
something that you
don't even look back

to want something you
can never have is to hold
hands with the wind

and yet i always knew this
wanting of you would be
the ending of me

still i stand here with my
hands full of wanting and
my heart full of you.

angie allen

begin again

somewhere
pressed
between
last chapter
and the end

i found
someone
who showed
me how to
begin again.

one life stand

one night just
wouldn't do
i want to spend
one life
maybe two
walking next to
someone like you.

angie allen

no place like home

remember when i told
you i wanted to go to kansas
so when we left i could say
we aren't in kansas anymore

i take it back i would settle
for the shoes the ruby red ones
and if only my shoes when clicked
could take me home to you

i wish i would have said that instead
maybe then you would have known
i could have made your heart my home
and now i can finally say it

we aren't in kansas anymore are we
maybe we never really were.

seeing is everything

sacrement

your lips are
full of words
i want to taste
like communion

to touch with
humbled hands
to repeat like
unsaid prayers.

angie allen

phased

in my dreams
i am whole
and we are us
and yet they
wonder why
i love the moon

it dreams me
whole again
if only in
phases.

seeing is everything

bi-lingual

scars speak
our stories
in native tongues
in hieroglyphics
of the heart

so speak to me in scars
it's a language i know well.

angie allen

...i will shatter
these windows

i will let the light in
i will make the way out
and when i do i can
promise you this
i will never again
be the girl in the box.

seeing is everything

the girl unboxed

there has always been something
unsettling about dancing ballerinas in boxes
you know the kind that only dance when
someone opens the lid
it never seemed right this idea of someone
determining when she came to life
someone telling her it was her turn to dance
but only at their discretion
it wasn't until i was older that i realized it
was a control mechanism
perhaps that was the underlying reason i
didn't care for the girl in the box because
in many ways i allowed myself to become her
i allowed others to dictate my every move
timing it with music of their own making
lids lifted on their queue
i have often heard it said when a door closes
a window opens yet i no longer care to test
that theory
i am about to scream so loud i will shatter
these windows i will let the light in
i will make my own way out and when i do
i can promise you this i will never again be
the girl in the box.

angie allen

revolving door

and that's the
difference
between
fantasy
and reality

we run from
one to hide
in the other.

seeing is everything

silent validation

i miss those quiet moments
saying nothing
not because we had nothing
to say but because we didn't
have to say anything

love doesn't always need
words to be felt
i miss those moments where
love was validated quietly.

angie allen

encore

we are walking amongst
a masquerade of the
broken and damaged
who hide shattered
hearts behind tired eyes
and storybook smiles

we are walking amongst
the oscar worthy
those playing the leading
role in their own lives

those saying smile
illusions sold here

and we applaud you with
roses on standing feet.

seeing is everything

a process

breathe
break
begin
again.

angie allen

sunflower

i will love until
i am heavy with sun

until i am more
petals than person

until i am soft.

seeing is everything

the thing with wings

i held onto hope
with borrowed breath
and swallowed silence

knowing feathers would
surely fall from my lips
if i were to open my mouth

in voice
in song
in protest.

angie allen

...you have my heart racing

love drunk and buzz worthy
over a set of friday night eyes
and i never saw you coming.

seeing is everything

love drunk & buzz worthy

enter you and i was all deer
caught in the headlights with a
didn't see you coming look about me
my mouth and heart wide open

and i was thinking thank goodness
for u-turns and do-overs because i was
anything but on track
a derailed mess of a thing and
you were looking for
anything but perfect

i was never one of those girls
with gifted penmanship
you know the kind that sailed off
pretty paper with back road curves
yet the very thought of you has me
thinking in cursive wanting to fold into
you like origami in deft hands

you have my heart racing
love drunk and buzz worthy
over a set of friday night eyes
and i never saw you coming.

angie allen

traitor

i feel alien in this
land of the broken
parts and home of
the used up hearts

whole is a rare
commodity
in a world of
skin and bones

yet the market
is always open
for trading.

seeing is everything

swallowed whole

i learned that in the silence
is where the most growth occurs
when i tucked myself in between
the spaces of my breath and i
released myself into the vastness
it would either do one of two things

swallow me whole or
make me whole again
over time i realized it would do
both sometimes simultaneously

to be swallowed and made whole
at the same time is a beautifully
surreal thing

you will know it when you know it.

angie allen

…the truth is

you never wanted to
know the full story

you simply wanted
to put your hands
on the pages.

seeing is everything

cliff notes

i try to take people at the capacity
they are willing to give
yet here's the thing about that
in order for it to actually work
there has to be something
in your hands there just does
that our perception is our
reality is a double edged sword
because we see what we want to see
and now i am seeing it for what it really is
albeit a little too late
the truth is you never really
wanted to know the full story
you simply wanted to put your
hands on the pages
in the end you were nothing more
than luke warm hands grasping
for the cliff notes - lazy.

angie allen

loneliness

they say necessity is the
mother of invention and
perhaps that is true
i've just come to realize
that loneliness is but a
shade away from necessity
oh what i've done under the
guise of loneliness for things
i was sure i couldn't do without

need, need, need

that feeling of needing others
will bleed you dry if you let it
i sit here today with a heart
bled out and a hand full of
needs too heavy to hold
not wanting to admit that
i need you still.

seeing is everything

the becoming

i had to fall a long
way from who
i was

in order to
become all that
i am

and oh
what beauty
there is in
the becoming.

angie allen

…let's make a mess

of a mess that's what real
love looks like anyhow
a big beautiful
freakin' mess.

beautiful mess

you and i we are just
two people hanging on
by the threads of who
we used to be
pressed for time the kind that's
never on our side
don't even get me started
on how the odds are stacked
against us
i know we don't have a shot in hell
but when did that ever stop love
when did that ever stop anyone
from fighting
and please for the love of god
don't tell me i'm better off without you
that's just the hurt talkin'
let's just forget the noise in our heads
and trust these broken hearts have more
miles in them than they're letting on

let's make a mess of a mess that's
what real love looks like anyhow
a big beautiful freakin' mess.

angie allen

seeing is everything understanding is power.

seeing is everything

spring

angie allen

eyes wide open

i used to watch my life
through spread fingers
at times not wanting to
see things for what they were
or maybe for who i was
maybe both and yet where's
the honesty in that

it wasn't until i stood back
stood still and saw things
for what they truly were
that's when the clarity came

if i know anything it is this
you can't unsee the things seen
once you see them for what
they are there is no going back

seeing is everything
understanding is power.

seeing is everything

grounded

break me
down to dust

eventually
but not today
not by you.

angie allen

…i was never meant
for small things i was
never meant for you.

seeing is everything

not for you

i couldn't quite put my
finger on it this feeling
that was growing inside of me
then a school bus rode
past me today and i thought
to myself yes that's it
when you are young school
seemed to swallow you whole
it seemed so huge
then when you are older
and go back to visit it seems
so very small like you don't
even remember it being that small
and that's just it the building
didn't change i did - i grew
what i'm trying to say is
being around you now is like
being in a school after you've grown
i was never meant for small things
i was never meant for you.

angie allen

taste test

oh to taste your
dark thoughts

if nothing more
than to know the
flavor of my name.

seeing is everything

fly

feathers are a reminder
that while we may lose
small pieces of ourselves
along the way flying isn't
about being whole
it's about being free.

angie allen

friends

my circle may
be small yet

i want stayers
not players.

seeing is everything

cupped

i hold hope
in my heart
like the moon
holds the light
of the sun

with both hands.

angie allen

look up

open your eyes
wide to the
universe

and it will open
it's infinite heart
to you.

seeing is everything

skinful thoughts

the mere thought
of you does me in

imagine if we were
skin to skin.

angie allen

...everything is now
until it isn't.

seeing is everything

now

the only thing that is real
that is tangible is
right here right now
moments in their beautiful
singularity are diluted to
a tiny word - now

everything is now

if this phrase is thought of
in the reverse as if to ask what
was before the here and now
it then becomes

now is everything

so make the most of
your now for it is
everything until it isn't.

angie allen

gifted

and still the
most beautiful
thing you ever
gave me was
butterflies.

seeing is everything

i miss you

in times
in seasons
in pieces

and yet on this
rainy october
morning, i find
i am missing you

in oceans.

angie allen

forever's edge

your lips take me
places without
zip codes and the
edge of forever
never tasted
so good.

seeing is everything

deft tones

if only my tongue
were autumn
and crisp winds

where words fell
in shades of saffron
and apricot

instead they collect
behind my teeth like a
sunday prayer swallowed
in the silence of winter.

angie allen

bibliophile

if you can read
me like a book
for the love of
god make it one
not so plainly read.

seeing is everything

rewind us

we were love once
we were love
we were
we.

angie allen

hollow

somedays i
feel more bone
than skin from
this darkness
that rages deep
within.

seeing is everything

broken whole

we can't
carry our
b r o k e n
and expect
to be whole.

angie allen

...it began to swell

inside of me like
a balloon with air
only it weighed me
down this living
breathing thing
this emptiness.

seeing is everything

weighted

i can't recall when
it began to spread
when it began to
consume me
when the silence
became so
altogether suffocating
it began to swell
inside of me like a
balloon with air
i could feel it moving
in between us
pulling me in
pushing you out
i could feel it take
on a life of its own
i was full
filling
overfilled
with nothing at all
only it weighed
me down this living
breathing thing
this emptiness.

angie allen

the unseen

i think that's
what love is like
this endless ability
to be both in the
moment and see
beyond it at the
same time
to see what isn't
always there.

seeing is everything

time keeper

in the end maybe
that's all i'll ever be
a collector of moments

if i've learned anything it is
despite wanting moments
to be *more than*
if we can appreciate that
they just *were* it's easier

we become conditioned to
expect more and yet sadly
even when we have the more
often times they aren't what
we expected them to be

so i'm back to moments and
in the end maybe that's all i
will ever be

a collector of moments.

angie allen

destroy me in love

i don't want to fall
into you softly

i want crashing waves
and thunder

walking against the wind
rain blowing sideways
fire and fury

i want a storm of
indescribable magnitude
to calm this screaming
restlessness inside of me.

seeing is everything

risk it all

i dove into this
heart first and
eyes wide shut

if blind is how we
know then know i
don't see anyone
but you

if chances are how
we know then know
i am risking it all

for what is life
without risk
what is love
without going
all in heart first
and eyes wide shut.

angie allen

reckless love

i want the
reckless
without the
abandon

let's call it reckless then.

seeing is everything

an awakening

i'm not sure i can rightly
explain how your words
feel more like memories
how they feel more like ours
less like yours

they feel every bit a part of me
like they aren't reaching my ears
for the first time

the only way to describe
it is to say i never believed
in love at first sight until your
words read like memories at
first glance

and maybe
that's what love is
a memory waiting
to be awakened.

angie allen

broken hearts still beat

it is unbelievably exhausting
holding on to a heart that
was never mine to hold in
the first place
so here i am letting go of
yours to salvage what is
left of mine
there is a breaking point
between the holding on
and the letting go
if you hold on until you break
you are forced to let go
if you let go before you break
then it's a release
one we have control over
the other has control over us
i've been on both sides
going forward i will ensure i
remain on the side that i control
if nothing more than to salvage
what is left of an already broken
but still beating heart.

seeing is everything

unfold

if my heart
were a flower
it would softly
whisper in your ear

pick me and watch
me unfold for you.

angie allen

…and like the

rain
leaves
stars
and tears

we must learn
to let go.

seeing is everything

beauty in the fall

like a beast of burden
we carry such weight
on our shoulders
such carnage in our ribs
lead in our hearts
unsaid words in our throats
nature is so cyclical and i can't
quite call it timing so let's call it
intuitive in knowing just when to let go

and like the
rain
leaves
stars
and tears

we must learn to let go
for you see there is such
beauty in the fallen is there not
such grace in the letting go.

angie allen

pushing up daisies

it was a rather
unspectacular day
nothing special
if i'm being honest

there was just
one small twist
unnoticed by
everyone but me

i woke up and
you were not
the first thing
i thought of

i smiled and
recalled this
flower i had
seen at the
park sunday

seeing is everything

it was a beautiful
daisy in the crack
of a sidewalk

despite the odds
she pushed her
way through rocks
and she made it

like a daisy that
blooms in sidewalk
cracks i pushed
through to the other
side of you

push through to
the other side of
where you are

if daisies can do it
you can too.

angie allen

seven deadly sins

i know it's
a sin to covet
one of seven
in fact

and yet here
i am wanting
all of you for
all of me
where's the
sin in that?

seeing is everything

migrating monarchs

my body used to
be a sanctuary to
your winged things

i'm not sure who
i miss more
the butterflies
or you?

angie allen

beautiful disaster

let's make
mayhem
and call it
magic.

seeing is everything

you a muse me

if the earth
laughs in flowers
then know
you are my earth
for i bloom
whenever
you are near.

angie allen

what if

oh the power of
two little words

breathe life to them

sometimes the smallest
of words can leave the
largest marks of all.

seeing is everything

taste

i want to taste
your darkness
lick it from your soul
drink it from your lips
fuck it from your mind
turn it into a work of
fiction so that every inch
of you is mine.

angie allen

no

on the other side
of a yes is a no

i found myself there
with them asking why
and me with

no reply, no reply.

seeing is everything

forever mine

i want to taste
shades of october
on your lips

unfold like spring
beneath your hips

feel summer's
heat from
your fingertips

as you trace
figure eights
across the
seasons of
my spine

for in that
way you will
forever be mine.

angie allen

… i haven't grown

this far
to simply
grow this far.

seeing is everything

keep growing

we are roots long
before we are stems
ages before we are flowers
i know it's a process
and there are days
when i simply want to stop
because the process
is too exhausting
and yet a voice from
within keeps telling me
i am where i am suppose
to be right here right now
that i haven't grown this
far to simply grow this far
i know it's true i have so
much more to grow
so much farther yet to go.

angie allen

time capsule

my heart still beats in analog
measuring love in
minutes & seconds
moments when time
lingered and i selfishly
wanted all of you in those
silent spaces between the
tic & toc
when we held our breaths in quiet
moments of static between the
needle & vinyl
before the record began to play
so forgive me if i stare
blankly at time pieces
press watches to my ear or
trace the ridges of records
i am merely recalling moments
when my heart measured
time with you.

seeing is everything

exercise of trust

these are the moments when
i tell myself i don't want to need
anyone anymore because it puts
me in the most precarious of positions
places of suspended animation
this wanting this needing

and then i come to and in the same
breath and in the same lucid thought
mutter *but i do i do need you.*

and i know asking you to trust
when trust is lying at your feet in
a million shattered pieces is like asking
for the impossible and yet i am

i am asking you to open wide the
doors of your heart and trust

in you
in me
in us.

angie allen

mourning routine

i want to bury
memories in
your mouth
find a place of
mourning before
your lips for surely
all else will smack
of emptiness after this.

seeing is everything

i wish

his eyes met mine
and when he
reached for me
i swear i saw
every star i ever
wished upon fall
from his very hand.

angie allen

chrysalis

self discovery is
holding beauty in
the palm of your
hand and seeing
the wings while the
rest still see the
caterpillar

find yourself
love yourself
see yourself
with wings.

seeing is everything

my two suns

it is altogether
peaceful

this silence
this unspoken
poetry

in the rise
and fall of
your chests.

angie allen

over you

i feared you would leave
as they always do and so
it was ironic how it was
me that left you

i always knew there
was no being me
if we stayed as two

for you see there
were two of me
the old and the new
and just one of you
just one of you

i was too much me and
you were not enough you

in the end i knew
you'd never do
you'd never do

in the end i chose me
over you.

seeing is everything

butterflies

i'm not concerned
with the ones that
got away
only the ones
meant to stay.

angie allen

heavy

there are days
when my heart
can not shoulder
the burden of an
almost.

seeing is everything

exhume

and yet
at times
the only way
to go higher
is to dig deeper.

angie allen

redeemed

it was the
way in which
the truth
washed over
me that i knew
i could begin again.

seeing is everything

winged things

i see you
in every
butterfly
wondering
if it once
graced my
stomach
with your
name on
its wings.

angie allen

p.s. i love you

if stars spilled secrets
your name would
literally be in lights.

seeing is everything

breakfast & you

things that taste
better in bed.

angie allen

...i wanted
something

that wasn't
yours to give
your heart.

seeing is everything

king of hearts

it has always been you
you just never stopped
long enough to realize it
this beautiful power you
held over me and still do
me with all of my intensity
and light
you with all of your broken
pieces and darkness
i never minded them
matter of fact they were
the parts of you that
spoke to me the loudest
sang the sweetest
were painted the brightest
you thought you would
only suck the light out of me
yet don't you realize the
sun sets on darkness only
to shine again
i really only wanted
one thing and yet that
something wasn't yours to give
your heart.

angie allen

saved

you're a pocket
full of maybes
on a rainy day.

seeing is everything

lost

i whispered
breadcrumbs
upon your lips
for i knew i was
going to lose
myself in you.

angie allen

...like all things perfect

*we were never
meant to last.*

seeing is everything

eden

merely moments
that is all we ever were
always one hello away
from a goodbye

i rarely use that word
as if there were a happy
way to depart with heart
in hand

and yet for you it was fitting
to be left alone in the end
you with your hands that

pushed and
pushed and
pushed away

i was perfect in your world
isn't that what you said
well perfection is for gardens
and beginnings and look
where that has gotten us

how fitting then that like
all things perfect we were
never meant to last.

angie allen

remember me not

we are constant shades of
remembering upon shades
of forgetting an ever turning
kaleidoscope between the two

if we are what we remember
and are also what we forget
would it not stand to reason that
we are a variation between the two

between the remembering and
forgetting there is this vast cavern of
in between and this is where we reside
pushing and pulling between the two

of the things we remember what of
that would we like to forget
how much of what we forget did we
desperately want to hold on to before
it made it's way out of reach
in this way we are constantly recreating
and refashioning who we were with who
we are and who we are yet to become.

seeing is everything

calculated love

funny the things people
tell you about love

what it is
what it isn't
how you know
when to stay
when to go

yet the one that always
gets me is 'be calculated'
is there even such a thing in love

i don't claim to have the answers
i do know this though
math was never my strong suit
so if love requires theories
and algorithms to figure it
the hell out then let's just
say my calculator only
functions at all or nothing.

angie allen

…tough days

for forever ways.

seeing is everything

tough days for forever ways

it was the way in which it rolled off
his tongue that made me taste the
hopeful flavor of freedom
to realize it was within reach - it was
feasible
tangible
palpable

i had to do the hard work - the bare
knuckled gut wrenching hard stuff
storms of fear were raging inside of me
and yet that is what fear does
it creeps into your creases but i would
not let it seep into my pores

i kept pushing at it until it
thundered and gave way
just enough to let the light in
just enough for me to know the way
was forward there was no going back
no retracing steps already taken
tomorrow lies in the western skies
i was going to make my way there
if only to stand in the origin of light
with the tough days behind i could
now begin a new journey to walk in
the face of new found freedom *forever.*

angie allen

in the end my scars were the wings that saved me.

seeing is everything

summer

angie allen

...in the end my

*scars were the
wings that
saved me.*

seeing is everything

my salvation

scars are time
travelers of sorts
bridging the gap of
where we have been with
where we have yet to go
they are the tellers of our stories
they speak without
having to say a word and
thankfully like any story
they remind us pain too
has an ending
that darkness eventually
yields to the dawn of day
to the place of new beginnings

we can begin again this
i know for sure because in the
end my scars were the wings
that saved me.

angie allen

high frequency

i'm drawn to
what i feel
rather than
what i see

you've got me
completely
high on your
energy.

seeing is everything

forever, eyes & windows

three things i
believe in with
all my might
for each
beautifully
holds
their truth
their light.

angie allen

magic

it was the way
he smiled that
made me wish
for snow in july
like anything
was possible.

seeing is everything

shine

today i swallowed
the sun so i could
be there for myself
when nobody else could

shine for myself.

angie allen

cramped

i am too
much heart
and you are
not enough
home.

seeing is everything

attainable

he said goodness had
been redefined for me

it was in that moment
i realized everything
literally *everything* was
within my reach.

angie allen

solo flight

let go of the pain
find your wings

paint the sky with
songs only your
scars can sing.

seeing is everything

discovered

amidst the
struggle
i found my
strength.

angie allen

nude awakening

you managed
to touch me with
no hands and

u n d r e s s e d

my mind with
your words.

seeing is everything

never look back

they said she
looked back
and became salt

i look forward
and know

i am salt
i am water and
i carry an ocean
inside of me.

angie allen

humble abode

give a woman
a house and she
will give you a
home they say

i say give me your
heart and i can
do the same thing.

seeing is everything

quite storm

i am drawn
to you like
eyes to a
window in
the dark of
a storm

a thing of
quiet chaos
a thing of
orchestrated
beauty

a thing spinning
so closely in front
of me and yet like
the horizon you are
too far away to
really touch.

angie allen

love me in braille

you do not need words
to be heard for even
in silence the heart speaks

you do not need hands to
be felt for even the thought
of you touches me in places
hands have never reached

and that is what love does
it speaks our language
without saying a word.

seeing is everything

i have a heart for in betweens

flowers in between pages
pauses in between kisses
small deaths in between life
moans in between sheets
comics in between the news
weeks in between summer and fall
small towns in between big cities
laughter in between tears
your fingers in between mine

beginnings and endings have their place
i just prefer the spaces in between.

angie allen

...i am still a giver
always will be

these days though i
am a guarded giver
it's how i know
who to share
my pieces with.

seeing is everything

guarded giver

the sign on my heart used to read
need a piece take a piece
have a piece give a piece
fashioned after the signs i sometimes
see by cash registers in gas stations

it's fitting really this idea of give and take
reality is there is rarely more than two cents
in those things because clearly there are more
takers than there are givers

i am still a giver always will be
these days though i am a guarded giver
my heart has a new sign too it reads
broken heart assembly required
honestly it works like a charm

the ones that read assembly required
and think this isn't what i signed up for
will leave every time

it's the ones that don't mind rolling their
sleeves up that stick around
in the end it's how i know who to share
my pieces with.

angie allen

oui, oui, oui

kiss me
until our
bodies make
love in french.

seeing is everything

sunrise service

if i'm being
honest if i'm
being true

i want to do
some devoutly
non-religious
things with you.

angie allen

jealous

i know its a peculiar
thing to be jealous of
those strangers that get to
steal glances and stares
the ones who get to share
the same breaths of air
or pass you by in the coffee
shops here and there

and maybe i'm just a little
jealous of all the ways the
world gets to hold you when
they don't even realize the
depth of who they have in
their hands.

seeing is everything

sparks

"you're glowing."

love, she said
that's what love does.

angie allen

cosmic lust

what's a girl
to do with
cosmic lust
when boys like
you taste of
whiskey and
stardust?

seeing is everything

autumn

and it was
the way my
clothes fell
at your feet
like leaves
that convinced
me you were
autumn.

angie allen

a haiku, empty stomach

my stomach would be
empty if you left and took
the butterflies too.

seeing is everything

shifting weight

fault lines shift
beneath the weight
of your words
unearthing truths
never seen before
never heard.

angie allen

weight over

when the wait we
carry in our ribs
is no longer worth
the weight it's time
to move on

from people
from things
from ideas
that weigh
us down

wait for it
for him
for her
for them

only you know
when the wait is
no longer worth
the weight.

seeing is everything

vantage point

light that was created millions
of years ago is just now reaching us
is just now allowing itself to
be seen for the first time
so in many ways we are loving at the
speed of light

this love that was formed long
before we were here
ages before we knew it
would reach us
has finally shown itself
in the here and now

it tells me we can not deny
who we are meant to be
love like light changes our perspective
changes our view

and now i believe in everything
again when i see the world from
your shoulders.

angie allen

…in the end truth

is what you believe
can one really claim
a monopoly on such
a thing?

seeing is everything

truth monopoly

we all have them these
things we believe in
some beliefs are so strong
those ones that run so deep
they are forever a part of us

i know this to be true it's what
makes each of us who and
what we are and adversely
who and what we are not.

we fight for them
take risks
love and hate
create for them
is there anything
we won't do for them

without beliefs what would we truly be
and so in the end truth can be just as
relative as the next relative thing

in the end truth is what you believe
can one really claim a monopoly
on such a thing?

angie allen

layers of me

home is everywhere
i have been and
everywhere i have
yet to go

love is everyone i
have met and
everyone i have
yet to know

somewhere in
between the
going and the
knowing are
all the versions
of me

who i was and
who i am yet
to be.

seeing is everything

love transcends

when you carry a
heart full of flames
within your ribs
that love remains inside you
burning and smoldering

your flames may die
with you and yet from
ash can a fire be woken
from embers love will
glow within you once again

and in that way love does
the seemingly impossible
it transcends.

angie allen

remains of the day

here in that singular
moment in time
directly on the horizon
when the sky yawns
and swallows the last
bit of sunlight

if i could hold the
remains of the day
in my hands and lips
i would press their
colors into the deepest
canyons of your soul

if nothing more than to
make those parts of
you feel less alone in
the dark.

seeing is everything

hummingbird heart

you've the heart
of a hummingbird
too large for the
body they gave you

is it any wonder
you grew wings

for how else were
you to carry the
weight of it all
with you?

angie allen

pluck you

his eyes were soft
they spoke in petals
and wavered between

i lust you i lust you not

i am more petals than
person soft in all the
right places, yet let's
be clear

i'm no plucking daisy.

seeing is everything

sinful smile

i want to
taste the
smile on
your lips

the one that
makes my
butterflies
flip.

angie allen

…i'm not asking
for much

*just say you'll
remember.*

seeing is everything

remember me

you asked me once what i saw
in you and i simply replied
everything you can't
see in yourself

it's always hard to see yourself in
somebody else's eyes you though
you were the worst and i can say that
with a slight laugh now

we were brief just a small passing in a
lifetime of moments yet we existed
together for a time all the same

and maybe that's all some of
us will ever be for another
moments until we are memories

i'm not asking for much just say
you'll remember
in the end i think that's
what each of us want

to be seen
to be loved
to be remembered.

angie allen

cosmic connection

when i'm with you
even the stars seem
to shine just a little
bit brighter.

seeing is everything

skeleton key

i keep all of
my dirty secrets
locked inside

so my skeletons
have company and
a dark place to hide.

angie allen

about last night

whiskey
dreamin'
over coffee
steamin'.

seeing is everything

unveiled

we were
dressed in
nothing but
the truth
and damn
it looked
good on us.

angie allen

blown

the only thing
i wanted to
blow was your
mind

first things first.

seeing is everything

pieces of us - a ghost story

these walls hold my peace like mouths
hold a prayer like veins carry a pulse
deep within so we are never without

your love awakened me
like an open
door to a shutting window
it consumed me

there are no four walls that can
contain our love and yet when you left
i had not choice but to leave my piece
here in this house inside the history of
these walls as if to say

we lived here
we loved here and
my heart beats here

it beat with you
it beat for you
and it will never beat
the same without you

wait for me here in this
house where we made
love our home.

angie allen

i fought the universe for you

what if all that i am brought
me here to all that you are
in this very moment

what if we've walked the
lines of love but they haven't
always been linear

you see you don't even
realize this but i fought
the universe for you

i once wrestled stars
just to trace the curve of
your lip then realigned them
so i could hear you say my name

seeing is everything

i've altered entire constellations
just to watch the rise and fall
of your chest

i've shifted the tides and altered
the force of gravity so i could fold
the pages of our story into the
paperback of your spine

and time when it didn't speak
our language i folded it's hands
backwards so i could press forever
into the salt of your skin

love yeah its linear and
then some and i should know
i fought the universe for it
i fought the universe for you.

angie allen

empty spaces

i feel you in between
heart beats the way i
feel the sun in between
shadows

your light fills my empty
with the spaces in between.

seeing is everything

inferno

your touch would
ignite something
from which i would
never recover
or so i would imagine.

angie allen

natural disasters

we need only look skin deep
to know we are made of dust

how painful a thing
to be so utterly human
to carry hairline
fractures in our bones
fault lines in words
hurricanes in our hips
we break and we break
and we break again

we spill our contents if
nothing more than to see
what we are made of
where we have come from
whose pieces we carry within us

yes i am dust but
i am also salt and water
and i carry an ocean
inside this skin
wind and waves
inside these bones.

seeing is everything

fear less, love more

i've really only
one thing left to
say and it is this

it's okay to fear love
and yet you can't avoid it
not forever anyhow.

angie allen

for the love of art

please let me
paint pictures
with my lips on
your skin

let me move your
heart in shades of
softness drawn in a
singular line of love

please let me
love you like art
let me be the score
you sing when love
pulls on your
heart strings

say you'll be linear
say you'll be love
say you'll be all
of the above.

seeing is everything

mind tapped

deft are the
tongues that
turn on
light bulbs
inside your head

leaves you
to wonder
what they
could do
inside your bed.

angie allen

...exit through
the gift shop

howl my truth
bare this badge proudly
lone party of wolf.

seeing is everything

lone party of wolf

i lost myself in their found
then found myself lost in a world
where happiness came with conditions
and fine print was the big print

i knew where i was and where i needed
to be and while i didn't know how i was
going to get there i knew i wanted
off the ride and out of the park

if they could love on their terms
i could leave on mine

i knew i needed to keep moving
keep questioning - question it all
and then don't bother to look back
it was a necessary exodus
by pass the closed doors
don't bother with the damn windows
i would find my own way out

in the end i would exit
through the gift shop
howl my truth
bare this badge proudly
lone party of wolf.

angie allen

living pieces of you

you and me
we are collectors
of moments

i know this
to be true

and i am grateful
for those few i've
collected here
with you.

seeing is everything

press play

you're the score
to my core
the music
in my mind
you're the one
i've had on replay
now for maybe
the thousandth
time.

angie allen

to do

i've this list
of all the things
i'd like to do
none of which
involve clothes
all of which
involve you.

seeing is everything

glasses, voices & cain

a few of my
favorite things
to raise.

angie allen

mind full

the universe
inside of your
mind creates
butterflies
inside of mine.

seeing is everything

full on empty

i love the way
we talk ourselves
empty and yet it
leaves us so full.

angie allen

...i know your heart

has been broken by all the
wrong hands in all the
right places.

seeing is everything

be impossible

i know your heart has
been broken by all the
wrong hands in all the
right places and it feels
next to impossible to
believe you will ever
be anything but broken
pieces of something
never given a chance to
be loved whole

it seems impossible to
believe this time will
yield a different result
but that's the thing about
the impossible - it is
impossible until it isn't
so yeah i am asking you
for the impossible

can you please just this
once be impossible with me?

Made in the USA
Columbia, SC
26 March 2019